The Second Best of
TARZANA JOE

The Second Best of
TARZANA JOE

Tarzana Joe

To order additional copies of this book, contact:
Xlibris
1-888-795-4274
www.Xlibris.com
Orders@Xlibris.com
779093

Contents

Foreword

Dear Readers (and listeners),

Thank you for nearly 20 years of allowing me into your homes, your cars, and your ears. On a fateful day, long ago, I was a caller to the Hugh Hewitt Radio Show. I offered my services as a renowned expert on the works of Shakespeare (I had read them) for a monthly segment Hugh was planning. I didn't get the gig. Fortunately, David Allen White of the United States Naval Academy got the job. I was offered an assistant professorship in Poetry. As someone who loves the sound of my own voice (ask my wife), I jumped at the chance. Once a month, on the morning edition of the show, Hugh and I discussed the life and works of a selected poet. It was fun…and I got to be on the radio!

Then, one February, a few days before Valentine's Day, I offered to write a love poem for any listener who might have procrastinated in purchasing a gift. I was flooded with emails. Oops. I have been writing poems ever since. In addition to the verses you may have heard me read on the air, I have written hundreds of wedding toasts, eulogies, anniversary, and birthday poems. I wrote a love poem for a three-star general and a love-letter to a family home that was being put up for sale.

Many of my clients say that my work moves them to tears. Funny, my friends used to say that about my singing.

It has been my pleasure to play word games with you for all these years and I am grateful that you decided to purchase this collection. Thank you for the opportunity to try to make you smile.

Tarzana Joe

Dedication

To my dear wife, the Fetching Tarzana Johanna,
who puts up with my rhyming all over the house
at odd times of the day and night.

Who am I?

Poets have a duty
As this poet's often said
To see the world around them
From inside another's head

To question all assumptions
And to challenge every truth
Which helps us do our duty
Which, you know, is saying sooth

And I attempt each Friday
Just within the broadcast hour
To practice my vocation
Which is speaking sooth to power

I go for inspiration
Anywhere the headlines lead me
In hopes the proud and powerful
Will hearken to and heed me

I use the art of rhyming
Mixed with humor as a tool
Dusting off my subjects with
Some gentle ridicule

Frankly, very recently
I'm feeling some frustration
As public figures practice…
Auto-immolation

I say this quite reluctantly
Though spoken with all charity
Folks are acting out absurdity
It's impossible to parody

Much of what I write about is political, though I do occasionally write about starry nights, hockey or potato salad. The general opinion is that the political discourse in the United States today is too angry and too loud. But I beg you to study history. When the stakes are high (and they are up there right now) the voices contending for influence are rightfully excited. The fight is not only for power but for the future. I am convinced that the ruthlessness around the 2016 election did not come from malice, but from firm convictions on both sides that victory was essential. The accusation is that some, acting from this deep belief, crossed legal and moral lines to ensure that their candidate prevailed. The media is part of the puzzle. Recently I was listening to a lecture on the Lincoln-Douglas debates. The historian made the point that it's hard to settle on a fair transcript of what the candidates said because the pro-Lincoln newspaper published an edited version that favored their candidate (and vice-versa). Should we be surprised that video recording is now selectively edited? But in all I write, I strive to encourage free speech and open debate…in hope, of course, that we achieve the outcome I desire.

We Are Family

To those who say we're finished
And our politics are broke
I say you lack perspective
And you just can't take a joke

We're one ginormous family
And like all fam'lies, fight
As one way toward arriving at
A sense of wrong and right

Contending for our country
And I think from coast to coast
The ones who laugh the loudest
Are the ones who love her most

Consider that opponents
Who don't think the way you do
Deep in their delusions…
Yet, they clearly love her too

And though it seems impossible
At compromise to meet them
A healthy change of attitude
Will help you to defeat them

Bury your amazement
That they ever got this far
And gently show the populace
What barnacles they are

So even when the rhetoric
Turns hard and rough and callous
Remember Father Abraham
Said none should harbor malice

And when you go to cast your vote
As campaigns reach the fall
Crush them at the ballot box
With charity for all

As much as I love a good debate, like many poets (think Byron) I am moody. There are days when I feel powerless to persuade. Perhaps it is because when we question ourselves, we can quickly access our own echo-chamber. It's right there on our phones. So, engage when you can. Standing too long in an echo-chamber can make you lose your hearing.

My Lefty Next-Door Neighbor

I think Bernie is a madman
And Ms. Clinton is a liar
But when I read this couplet
I'm just preaching to the choir

What she did deserves indicting
And I'm mad because she *ain't*
While my lefty next-door neighbor
Thinks the lady is a saint

He's a Hillary disciple
And a Sanders devotee
He thinks speech should be restricted
And that college should be free

If the sun is up there shining
Or some clouds are out there storming
I perceive it to be weather
While he calls it global warming

We hurl barbs across the hedges
And at loggerheads we tweet
And despite my slick summations
Our two minds will never meet

At one time a man's opinion
You could sharpen, shape and hone

But today it's more than likely
That opinion's set in stone

I recall a different outlook
When it wasn't just this way
And a person saw the sageness
In perceiving shades of grey

When a difference of opinion
Made you open for discussion
Not a slender thread of deference
From contusions and concussion

It's so clear it should be gospel
That no matter how one tries
You can read the Book of Wisdom
But that "*do not*" make you wise

So, if you're in Tarzana
And you hear a poet cursin'
It's because I've been unable
To persuade a single person

But still we try….

Words Won't Hurt

I am a man of many words
They are my bread and butter
I count a day successful by
The number that I utter

Some words are worth a dollar
Others, like, a quarter
And words are quite compelling
Written in the proper order

Great words can be the difference
Between defeat and winning
And words got all this started
Back, you know, in the beginning

But when, because we disagree
My Facebook friends assail me
I just stare at my keyboard
Because, my friends, words fail me

I don't know how to reach you
Deep in that pit of hate
What crime have I committed
When I want my country great

I'm not a mindless lackey
Or some evil madman's minion
The only rift between us
Is a difference of opinion

Promote the things you value
Speak out as is your right
Keep trying to persuade me for
Perhaps, one day you might.

But listen to my message
Before you blast and blame
Extend me just the courtesy
That I might do the same

If not, our future's shaky
I feel it in my bones
And words might be forgotten
Replaced by sticks and stones

To say I return to the same theme often is no exaggeration. We live to communicate. We marvel at the coordination of an ant colony and though we have slightly larger brains, it often appears we are unable to communicate as effectively. In this poem, I also offer a short review of a well-received movie.

Shhhhh

With every conversation now
No matter where I'm talking
I watch my words so carefully
It's like on eggshells, walking
I say, "The sky was clear last night
This weather sure is splendid."
Lest any other topic leave
My listener offended

Of course, such idle chit chat
Could be slammed as climate norming
And crass insensitivity
To fans of global warming

We can't speak of our favorite teams
Or rosters that we chose
I've seen how even Steeler fans
Can quickly come to blows

Things that once united us
Have now become a wedge
Who, in conversation, notes
The anthem or the pledge

You can't discuss the movies
Your friend downloads or rents
Especially "3 Billboards"
(Which isn't worth two cents)

There's hardly any avenue
To show and share your views
Considering it's hard to know
Which pronouns you can use

It seems, alas, that everyone's
Been put on the defensive
Pending each decision
On what Twitter deems offensive

So, with the understanding
That one word could start a riot
I think we'd all be served
By taking turns at keeping quiet

My plan could be the best thing yet
Or it might be the worst
So let's all take the silent vow
Go ahead, you first

I really didn't mean it. I want to hear from you. <u>tarzanajoe@hotmail.com</u>

Speak UP

In youth, I was reminded
To watch my Ps and Qs
And give consideration
To every word I choose

My Uncle Rocco warned me
The world was full of dangers
"Don't talk about the fam'ly
Like that in front of strangers."

So, I was always mindful
To measure every joke
And weigh all consequences
At length, before I spoke

Now if you gave that credence
There's more I'd like to tell you
And somewhere out in Brooklyn
There's a bridge I want to sell you

I never hesitated
Before I had my say
And probably said things
That are prohibited today

I likely said, "God Bless You"
Back when I was a kid
Because that was a kindness
That everybody did

But if we say, "Gesundheit"
Or tweet that "Jesus Saves"
Scores will say that they can't wait
To Polka on our graves

They'll dig up every essay
You wrote in junior high
To prove that you're a rotten girl
Or really, rotten guy

Now you might think my poetry
Is aimed in the direction
To recommend and advocate
A lot more circumspection

To pause at every crossroad
And choose the road not taken
If that's what you concluded
You are horribly mistaken

Unless to the tyrannical,
Our future you've resigned
I urge you to stand up to this
And freely speak your mind.

The first defenders of Free Speech should be the national media. But as you select from station to station (I was going to write "turn the dial") you will find that everyone seems to be saying the same thing. It is as if there is one place where the approved narrative is decided. The news has become like processed cheese.

Meet the Press

Creatures, whether great and small
That lack some introspection
Suffer from a process we call
Natural Selection

And in that sense, some journalists
Of dignified distinction
Like sabretooths and dinosaurs
Are heading for extinction

Where once three smart reporters stood
You'll see what's left of three bodies
With no one there to hand them any
Pulitzers or Peabodies

They all believe they toe the line
Of probity and fairness
Which shows that they're all missing
Just a little self-awareness

They sure like to pontificate
To lecture and expound
And think whatever leaves their lips
Is witty and profound

I know this weakness very well
The damage it can do
For I admit before you now,
I suffer from it too

Perhaps they're just too pretty
As everyone can see
Alas, again, I must admit
The same applies to me

They fail to differentiate
What's false from what is true
And as a certain consequence
They know not what they do

Whether you write poetry
Fight wars or knit a sweater
Most folks approach the tasks ahead
By trying to do better

Their weakness isn't vanity
Or arrogance or lying
The sad fact of the matter is
These folks aren't even trying

Just a Bill?

When I'm feeling worried
I spend those troubled nights
Counting up my blessings from
Our country's Bill of Rights

The document that states the things
Beyond the rulers' reach
Are freedoms of assembly
Worship, press and speech

It further goes to say
That there shall be no circumvention
Of rights our famous framers
Didn't list or failed to mention

And from the oldest justice
To his young amanuensis
It may be the one document
About which there's consensus

Everyone agrees, without a doubt
It would be wrong to
Retaliate against me for a
Group that I belong to

And who, besides some radical
Would write, opine or teach
My attitude on Climate Change
Should limit my free speech?

On campuses, I'm told I can
Say anything I please
From 3 to 4 on Fridays
If I do it from my knees

So, when I count those blessings
And my rights and their safe keeping
Is it any wonder that
I'm having trouble sleeping

A last word on free speech…I am not a conspiracy theorist. Oh, I know that conspiracies exist in the world; but we did land on the moon. And yet, it's not just the daily talking points that seem coordinated. There are ripples that indicate a steady, if not organized presence behind the long game the Left plays.

Mysteries and Conspiracies

We grapple with great mysteries
"What makes a saint or sinner?"
But the deepest question that we ask
Is often, "What's for dinner?"
We like to set the style
We live to make the scene
But nothing is so comforting
Quite like the old routine

Each morning when I think of work
Make my bed and suit up
I just want to be certain
My computer's *gonna* boot up
The price of gas will be increased
The sun keeps rising in the east
If you prick me, I will bleed
That's a Californian's creed

And though I think I know what's what
The evidence is mounting
There's more that I'm not sure of
Than the stuff on which I'm counting
Today they're all condemning
Who just yesterday was "god"
The mighty fall in moments
And I find that rather odd

When you put up a statue
You stick it in cement
You don't think, in a week or two,
You'll wonder where it went
Things like these teach old and young
To close their minds and hold their tongue
Issues cannot be discussed
Cause no one knows who they can trust

I don't treat with conspiracies
But I can tell you, man
No one may be plotting
But this sure looks like a plan

...and now for a little change of pace. From time to time (perhaps once a year) I write a poem about something other than politics. In 2017, I passed a kidney stone. It made a big impression on me. It was the first deep space object to show up on NASA's Asteroid Intercept Radar and barely missed the Yucatan peninsula.

Joe Passes and Throws the First Stone

Of all the pleasures I have known
One is NOT a kidney stone

It makes a person curse and swear
In language that I shall not share

But I'd take this for all my crimes,
Than read the *bleedin'* New York Times

Or lose to teams I hate the most
Than say I read it in the Post

I'd rather put aside my pen
Than watch a night of CNN

Or writhe as from a serpent's bite
Than see the nightly news each night

Since I'm in pain, though not quite dead
All I can do is shake my head

And though it isn't apropos
Another thing that you should know

I'd rather pass a string of pearls
Than watch an episode of "Girls"

When the holidays roll by, you can always count on Tarzana Joe for help. Following is my gift to the romantically challenged.

St. Generic's Valentine Poem

Each year my happy clients
Kindly offer me the chance
To help them with their words of love
As they pursue romance

They tell me who they're pining for
And then, I make some guesses
For, though I've never seen them
They are all my Beatrice-es

The custom poems I write
Can be sublime and atmospheric
But those of you who waited
Will be getting this generic…

Dearest love, I hardly know
The way to make a start
To tell you all the passion that
I'm holding in my heart

Your lips are jewels, your laughter light
Your smile, warm and rare
You set my soul on fire with…
(The color of your hair)

And though I'm not a scholar
When I'm with you, I am wise
For I've learned the subtle wisdom in…
(The color of your eyes)

Poets say that love is blind
Which raises the alarm
I'll never see another
As I'm blinded by your charm

But I don't care if I can't speak
Or smell or even see
For the only thing I know is
You're the only one for me

So, offer me a hopeful nod
Perhaps a welcome glance
Telling me O! (NAME GOES HERE)
My hopes have half a chance.

Dorothy Parker once said, "I hate writing. I love having written." Emile Zola once said, "I go to my work every day like a grocer." I have no idea what they were talking about and I prove that in my next poem.

Procrastination

Of all the words of tongue and pen
That bring a person sorrow
I think, by far, the cruelest are
"I'll get to it tomorrow."

For whether you are free from want
Or find yourself in need
"Tomorrow" is the single thing
That no one's guaranteed

It only takes an instant
To destroy what's stood for years
That goes for homes and nations
Reputations and careers

So, if you hear your partner say
"I'll do it in the morning"
Remember some disasters come
Without a moment's warning

And when the morning after comes
The ones that well have fared
Are scouts who know the wisdom
Of their motto, "Be Prepared"

Promise every day to do
The best a person can
And know that every evening
You are good with God and man

Organize your efforts
In the way your wife insists

Nothing helps the mem'ry more
Than making notes and lists

Your most important papers
Have you stored them safely, mister?
Scan them to a flash drive
And then send it to your sister

Here in California
There's a tip I always use
Glasses on your nightstand
And your wallet in your shoes

Don't be like this guy I know
The worst procrastinator
Now I've got some poems to write...
I think I'll do them later

A Short Poem, Long on Good Advice

Never try to be the guy
Who wonders what the use is
Believe that you can win a hand
With just a pair of deuces
So long as you don't waste your time
In making up excuses

Before we get political again, perhaps we should get spiritual. I was born a Roman Catholic and remain a church-going Roman Catholic. I have faith in a creator God who loves his creation. I believe the Bible contains great wisdom (and I should read it more closely and more often). I pray for grace and forgiveness. I strive, and I fall short. I hope that, in the end, I am not found wanting.

Easter

Reflecting on this moment's fears
My thoughts go back two thousand years
I think of how it happened then
The Judge of all was judged by men

Condemned because he spoke good news
And charged as king; King of the Jews
Yet in his heart he held no wrath
He chose to walk another path

So I, for one, will do my part
To emulate His Sacred Heart
Regardless where the times have brought us
To love, just as the Savior taught us

To conquer all the hate and lies
And, living his example...Rise.

After every great loss in our country, whether by natural disaster or the hand of man, many are moved to offer their thoughts and prayers. Recently, those who think little of prayer (and perhaps less of thought) have belittled those expressions of kindness. Here are two poems in response.

Prayer

If you've just read the Daily News
You're probably aware
Its editors are skeptical
And don't think much of prayer

They've had enough of platitudes
Of homilies and preaching
And say they'll gladly do without
So much of this beseeching

The quiet moment when a soul
Asks God to help another
Is clearly inefficient
So forget about it, brother.

And though they like to criticize
When other folks get preachy
They've climbed in to the pulpit
And, by God, their pushing Nietzsche

Progressives also offer prayers
You've heard it and you've seen it
The Daily News must understand
That they don't really mean it.

Behind the scenes they laugh a lot
Oh you should hear the zingers
They hurl at the believers
And the prayers and the clingers.

25

They think the act of prayer itself
A futile, vain endeavor
While, clearly to the rest of us,
We need more prayer than ever

Now, if you've thought about these things
You've likely heard the saying
God, by prayer, may not be changed
But change comes to those praying

Prayer cannot be measured
By good fortune, health, or wealth
The value of the prayer
Is in the act of prayer itself

Back when I learned Catechism
Lesson number two
Was, "Prayer is when you talk to God"
In grace, he talks to you.

The thing about this whole affair
The Daily News is missin'
You'll never hear the Word of God
Unless you stop to listen

Thoughts and Prayers

I hope you never suffer from
An attitude like theirs
The folks who show contempt for those
Who offer "thoughts and prayers"

Let me just assure them
That we know our poor petitions
May have but little power
To affect the world's conditions

We offer them in person
By a tweet, or on the phone
To let our fellow man know that
In this, they're not alone

To signal some assurance
At a catastrophic hour
There is a hand to help you
And there is a higher power

Although I know that some of you
May find it all dismaying
As long as suns keep rising
We're *gonna* keep on praying

The thoughts and prayers we offer
Will assume their proper place
When thoughts turn into action
And prayers turn into Grace

I will let this poem stand for itself (except to say that of all the poems I have written, I really like this one).

Our Time Has...

I wake
I work
I wonder
What sets the day's design?
Is this the last sun that you'll see
Or is the last look mine?

Did we, before creation
Watch as the clock was set
And like the great Greek in the poem
Accept the time we get?

Do we all sign the bargain
The mix of joy and strife
Aware that we must make the most
Of our allotted life?

And then, by some distraction
Forget along the way
That once we were aware
Of both the hour and the day

And in that frightful moment
Before the bill comes due
Does the soul, in sorrow say,
"I knew, I knew, I knew."

There is no consolation
A word then to the wise
The ending may be sudden
But it comes as no surprise

The lesson may be common
But its wisdom, unsurpassed
Live well, and live each day, my love
As if it were your last

As for the institution of the church itself, local or universal, a reckoning
has come and will keep coming until a better Jerusalem is built.

A Believer

It's far beyond my competence
And some may find it odd
To justify, As Milton might
The ways of Man to God

Since mankind first awakened
We sought to understand
Our place in this creation
That the great Creator planned

We sought it in the river
And we sought it in the wild
We sought it with the innocence
And wisdom of a child

We knew that in the thunder
And the bellow of the bear
Was something greater than we were
And sought to find it there

We found tremendous forces
That were fearsome and benign
And set our growing powers
To divine what was divine

We tamed the flooding river
And we caught the racing wind
Built ourselves a tower
And in doing so, we sinned

Coming from the rubble
We determined to be stronger

And we *builded* a cathedral
That would last a little longer

It stood for many centuries
It told the human story
As we filled it with our music
And imagined what was glory

But by the might of miracles
Its builders have been led
Its corridors neglected
And its followers, all fled

The cornerstone is lost, alas
The roof is old and leaking
And man is like a child again
Wandering and seeking

I claim no jot or tittle
No syllable or letter
But every time a tower falls
Let's aim to build it better

The start of the rebuilding is a commitment to kindness. The past few years have seen so many mass tragedies that it is difficult to know how to respond. Some are natural disasters and many more are man-made. We accept their challenge to be better in any crisis and especially when facing the final one.

Hello, Central...

The phone rings and somehow you know it's not good news
We all have so much and so much to lose
Hello, you say bravely to the night
Wishing you were wrong
But you were right.

Your mother isn't doing well
Her doctor told you Time will tell
But neither has that bedside touch
And neither really tells you much

At my age though, it's now a trend
Remember Pete, your high school friend
I don't know but his sister said
She went one night and found him

Surrounded or by all, neglected
Nearing, nigh, or unexpected
Suffering or in relief
We find ourselves alone, in grief

But when it comes, at once, for crowds
When there are shortages of shrouds
When darkness roars and clouds descend
Beyond what we can comprehend

Although it goes against the grain
Find comfort in the common pain

There's power in a little prayer
But more in one so many share

Here is a chance to understand
To give your blood or give your hand
Create the world you want to see
Be kinder than you have to be

Be thoughtful and stop thinking twice
When you have the chance, be nice

So, if you're called
And go tomorrow
The world will get the call with sorrow
And when that wretched phone stops ringing
All you'll hear is angels singing

Sometimes, angels cry. A guerilla news organization went undercover to discuss purchasing body parts from a group that advocates reproductive choice. There was righteous horror....from the news media....that any group would go so low as to deceive worthy scientists and doctors by such nefarious means and secretly record such talk. The groups claimed the videos were selectively edited and the issue faded. Perhaps there is no way to persuade on this topic, but perhaps...

Those Videos...and now our next story

Every builder knows
Who builds with wood or brick
No roof can be too sure
No wall can be too thick

A movement of the earth
Or accident of men--
That place the building stood
Is empty once again

A potter with his kiln
A sculptor with his hand
They know what they invent
Can soon be dust and sand

They strive with each creation
To fill a higher need
No challenge is worth taking
If you're sure that you'll succeed

For poets, it's the same
With all our brains and bluff
At times, we understand
That words are not enough

So, I have now to fashion
The words that I can say
To make a person see
When I must look away

The brokering of flesh
The bartering of blood
We crawled out of the ooze
To wallow in the mud?

We're specks in time and place
Oh! That is absolute
Why must we work so hard
To make life more minute?

A person's right to choice
Is something we can't lose
But tell me there's a heart
That would this horror choose.

I know there are no words
To make a mountain cry
But hear me if you can
At least I had to try.

"Choice" and progressive social justice are such passionate causes for so many that it seems anyone with a different point of view is deemed unworthy of debate. When debate is attempted, it appears that social justice rage gives the progressive unlimited power to dismiss their opponent from discussion (or from the planet). Really?

Would you and why?

Would you if you could without consequence destroy me
For the brutal injustice of my birth and the color of my skin?
If I called you brother
And felt you brother without fear
Would you still feel the need?
What then can I do?
Lay my neck and meager fortune on the ground?
Or walk away to somewhere unseen
Unoffending
Some island of shame
If not
If neither
Then what?
I cannot undo what centuries have done
Not what men like me have done to men like me
Not what men like you have done to men like you
Because we are all men and all men have done this.
Better together to make things better
But it is for you to decide
And if I am wrong.
If the anger is not hate
Tell me
Would you if you could…
and why?

Shall we return to politics? OK, let's. More and more, every election is portrayed as "the most important in our lifetime". This statement is unusual in that in many ways it is nonsense, and, in many ways, it is true. History is the best judge of the importance of an election; but each election sets the future on a path that history eventually deciphers for our descendants. I kicked the election cycle off for 2016 in this poem by throwing down the gauntlet…well, it was more like a golf glove… but you get the idea.

Now

There is a time, in men's affairs,
To face those dragons in their lairs

A time, when after introspection
We move things in the right direction

To know what north is and what south is
And put *yer* money where *yer* mouth is

A time for hate, a time for love
A time persuade evolves to shove

A time for niceties…
A time for nasties…
(I read that in Ecclesiastes)

The point I'll make, if you'll allow
I think that time and tide is now

We want something; so do you
A child knows what we should do

You want more, and we want less
There is a middle way, I'd guess

When I was young, I thought it wise
To learn the art of compromise

For give and take, the sages said
Is one way all can move ahead

You get gold, but pay the price
Then we shake, and all make nice

So, let us know the way you feel
There's lots of room to make a deal

The other option you can choose
That's "we win" – "you lose"

At the beginning of the election process in 2015, it seemed as if everything was about to unravel. Then, it did. Congress didn't seem to know how to act and the President was running the country with a phone, a pen, and a three-hole punch. The natives were restless. So was I.

Speak Softly, Mr. Speaker

When we should be growing stronger
Our position couldn't be weaker
Who'd have thought we'd all be saying
Sayonara to the Speaker

There was just a little difference
In the way our factions think
You believe that you're effective
And the base believes you stink

Yes, the freshmen have been restless
And the old guard have been griping
The bloggers have been vicious
And the pundits have been sniping

But it's not supposed to happen
Parties need to be united
Speakers don't resign
Unless, of course, they've been indicted

It's not like there are issues
Or the planet's in a crisis
With markets in a meltdown
Or the Russians "fighting" ISIS

Iran just ran us ragged
And the DOD's been hacked
If it's House of Cards we're playing
Then the deck is clearly stacked

So, consider me a cynic
But the way it seems to be
The whole thing's being run
Like it's reality TV

Great men are making speeches
And their noble goals pursuing
Then they take a break for cocktails
And it's really nothing doing

Now we watch as they maneuver
And it's always quite a trip
As they fight to be the one
That gets to steer the sinking ship

Well, the best laid plans of Congress
Often wither and unravel
We won't know what we've got
Until the guy picks up the gavel

We're stuck then with the leadership
The hand of fate anoints
I'd feel so much more content to
Bet the Browns and give the points.

Notice the reference to "reality TV" in the seventh stanza? Could I have seen something (or someone) coming? Probably not. I just needed six syllables. But then, there's this from early in the campaign. Well, not that early, because, as you will read, he had already destroyed his chances three or fours times before this poem was written. Now, I like to think the title was ironic.

It Will Never Happen

His hair is awful messy
His skin is awfully thin
If I could make a wager
Then I'd say he won't get in

Gadzooks and Gloriosky!
I guess I had it wrong
But based on that announcement
I predict he won't last long

Oh sure, the early polling
Has got him at the top
But by this time next Thursday
Bet you'll see those numbers drop

Alright, I was mistaken
Listen friends, it's only June
We've seen a hundred candidates
Who launch and peak too soon

And now he's really done it
Disparaging a hero
When polls come out tomorrow
His numbers will hit zero

Hello and stop the presses
His lead has gotten bigger

I really can't explain it
Remarkable. *Go fig'r.*

He doesn't have the programs
The temperament or tone
He said things that the media
Won't stand for or condone

So, friends, the guy's *finito*
I'm certain this is it
He's cracked another threshold?
Did Washington just spit?

When asked a tricky question
While cruising on his yacht
As part of his reply
He labelled "you know who" a "what"?

He may not be a genius
He may be wound too tightly
But folks who put up buildings
Should not be taken lightly

And now we're making pledges
And hearing fresh excuses
Oh, please don't make me think about
Know Nothings or Bull *Mooses*

The guy's a force of nature
A wrecking ball, a smarty
Be careful in the GOP
You might be the third party

The campaign moved along as most campaigns move. Rubber chicken. Talking points. Boredom. And the daily dose of political-speak which is the art of saying nothing in a way that nobody believes it.

The Lie Detector

No, I'm not a lie detector
But can tell without much trying
When a politician's speaking
It's a good chance that they're lying

Some will ask us for forgiveness
In our judgments, to be lenient
For it's hard to be forthcoming
When the truth is inconvenient

And today it's clear and common
In a politician's biz
That the truth can be quite awful
And it very often is

Thus, a confident assertion
Is beyond all jurisdiction
What you say is seen as truthful
If you say it with conviction

And a falsehood is strategic
So successful you can't beat it
For a lie becomes less heinous
With the more times you repeat it

But the problem with this method
As we all learned in our youth
If you lie with every answer
You can lose track of the truth

If you're honest, recollections
May be hazy and *ephemery*

Whereas liars have no option
But to have a darn good memory

For the pure prevaricators
To maintain their wiggle room
Must endeavor to recall precisely
What they said to whom

And no matter how they practice
And no matter what they sell
With a wink or with a gesture
They all leave a little "tell"

Our ability to spot them
Will advance and keep improving
If we discount every sentence
Spoken when their lips are moving.

Things really began to heat up with the tedious progress of the Clinton E-Mail Investigation. I put that in CAPS because I felt like it. Once again, we heard the familiar defense, "They're all out to get me." At bottom, this was an investigation (of sorts) of Hillary Clinton's efforts to circumvent the Freedom of Information Act by setting up a private server. I will point out for those not paying attention, that she did not just use non-government e-mail; she went to considerable expense and effort to set up a personal server and email system. She only overlooked the need to keep it secure. I think that if any minds were changed about Hillary Clinton, it was not because she may have violated a criminal code but because of her poor judgement in the whole affair. The next-to-last stanza is one of my personal favorites.

How to Get Away With

It's happening all over
Just like, you remember when
The vast right-wing conspiracy
Is on the move again

They've got their pitchforks sharpened
And their banners all unfurled
To see if they can stop
The smartest woman in the world

Their motives may be many
But their tactics are revealing
They just don't want a woman
Crashing through that Crystal Ceiling

The campaign clouds have gathered
And when it pours, it's *rainin'*
So now it seems for certain
That she'll have to do some *'splainin'*

I've done my best to save her from
Conservative abuses

By working out and offering
Some plausible excuses

She could just come out swinging
But not with crude or crass words
"I would have used department mail
But I couldn't recall my passwords"

She could play contrite and thoughtful
If she wants another take
"Yes, I'm sorry that this happened,
But what difference does it make?"

At last I think I've figured out
Her most effective play
If I were Mrs. Clinton
Then here's what I would say.

"The subjects were so sensitive
I couldn't take a chance
So I had a secret server built
In Sandy Berger's pants."

There, I've made a few excuses
And there could be many more
Or I guess that she could use a few
That she has used before.

She Had it in the Bag

They say that love is blind, my friends
But politics is blinder
Forgive me if you've heard this
But we all need a reminder
Whenever someone mentions
It's all over but the shouting
Remember the old adage
That there's benefit in doubting

It took a few years for people to appreciate "What Happened?. If you read Mrs. Clinton's book, you have her answer. Here is mine

John Moss; Father of the FOIA

For want of a nail
A shoe was lost
And down came a kingdom
At a mighty cost

The breeze that begins
With a butterfly's wings
Is the unobserved cause
Of appalling things

You say that's true
And I say so be it
So here is the story
The way I see it

Back in the sixties
Some of those in charge
Saw that the government
Was way too large

It meant, to them
There was trouble brewing
If the People didn't know
What the State was doing

So, a man named Moss
(It's a little-known fact)
Proposed the Freedom
Of Information Act

It didn't take skill
Or astute clairvoyance
That the bureaucrats saw this
As a big annoyance

But LBJ
Taking pen in paw
Signed the FOIA
Into law.

And by that act more often than naught
With many a case in a courtroom fought
Many abuses in the act were caught

And then, my friends
In a moment of fate
A woman at the head of
The Department of State
Who fitness, faith and foresight lacked
Decided to subvert
Mr. Moss's Act

That was the wingbeat
That was the nail
That was the folly
Of appalling scale

That was the whimper
That was the bang
Think for a moment
And you'll say, "Dang!"

For Mr. Moss
It was a great big win
But just the beginning
Of this mess we're in

Sorry if I jumped out of the campaign chronology. Those poems just seemed to go together.

I think what propelled Donald Trump forward was a general disgust with the way government pushes people around. That separated him from the other Republican candidates. Hillary's message seemed to be, "we won't push you around as much, "or, "we'll leave you alone and push other people around." The country, after Obamacare, wasn't buying. Trump was saying, I'll push the government around for you.

When Comes the Revolution?

When will we rise in passion
Oh, what will bring the day?
Could it be when the Leadership
Can tell us what to say?

Or will the barque of tyranny
At last begin to sink
That fateful day the Leadership
Can tell us what to think
(Just as they set the quota
On the ounces we can drink)

Or will their rise to power
Be forced to slow retreat
The moment that the Leadership
Can tell us what to eat

They say that they're for choices
But we've lost the right to choose
The comments we can favorite
Or the bags that we can use

The butter in our baked goods
Is in line for confiscation
They're *monit'ring* our messages
And even our lactation

If we don't stand tomorrow
I'm afraid it's our own fault
We should have seen this coming
When they came to seize our salt

So, will their codes and dictates
At last meet with repeal
The hour that the Leadership
Can tell us what to feel?

I did it as a child
But now that I am old
I vow to tell the Leadership
I won't do what I'm told

As it became clear that Donald Trump would be the nominee of the Republican Party, operatives had to scramble to dig up the dirt. I think all the termites had been assigned to Jeb! and Marco Rubio because no one in Hillary's circle imagined that The Donald would be The Candidate. Of course, their job was not a tough one. Trump had a trail of marriages and financial dealings that were sure to provide enough dirt to defeat him. It did...and it didn't. The heat would have scared off or destroyed any other candidate; but Trump always got by on results. He fixed the ice rink. He built the building. He got things done. When Joe the Plumber, a regular guy on the campaign trail, challenged Obama with a question about business taxes in 2008, the creatures of the swamp dug up a tax lien and questioned his plumbing license. It was a disgusting signal to anyone else who might think of raising an issue with the political and powerful. Joe the Plumber didn't have the tools or the personality to fight back. He was a little guy that bureaucrats could squash or shut up. However, The Donald was not. (at least, not at the time of this book's publication)

Privacy

They're storing all our emails
Each and every text
Calls are all transcripted
God only knows what's next

What girls wrote in their diaries
And each Cath'lic boy confesses
Is parked through perpetuity
In digital recesses

Soon video will recognize
And bureaucrats record
The books that I've been reading
And the way I praise the Lord

Then if I raise my voice
And they don't like my rants and railings

They'll summon up the database
That archives all my failings

They'll leak to friendly media
That I use swear and slack words
And on some rare occasions
Put my underwear on backwards

They'll whisper that it's easier
And would I like to try it
To go along with what they want
And keep my yapper quiet

That's what the deep state's doing
That's what the deep state's done
And if you hadn't noticed it
A war has just begun

Some guy deep down in records
Whose rep's too low to hurt
Just got the nod and signal
To go and leak some dirt

They think that this electorate is dumb
Or even dumber
They're treating Donald Trump
The way they treated Joe the Plumber

Well Joe didn't have the stinger
To bite back at the buzz
He didn't have the nation
But I think Donald does.

The Clinton e-mail saga dragged on. Surprisingly, Bernie gave her some cover when he said, "Enough with the e-mails." So did I. Sort of. Hey, you do the math.

Enough About Emails

My boss got very angry
You would think it was a crime
He caught me checking emails
On what should have been his dime

Now every time he sees me
He greets me with a glower
Ya' think he knows I stop
To check my Facebook twice an hour?

I should have spoken up
And told that boss man to relax
To read or write an email
Takes 5 minutes at the max

And at the most
I read or write a couple every day
The emails in my archive
Aren't close to 30 K

But then I got to thinking
Thirty thousand is a lot
The more I thought about it
Then, the angrier I got

Before I get my hackles up
And move my soul to wrath
I like to pause a moment
While I stop to do the math

Thirty thousand emails
Dealt with yoga and a wedding?

If each one takes five minutes
Then you know where this is heading

Go and crunch the numbers
And this is how it plays
To read that many emails
Takes a hundred and four days

That's quite a lot of wasted time
There should have been a warning
No wonder she didn't answer
When that phone rang in the morning

If I spent that much time at work
Racking up a debt
My boss would have a right to be
A little bit upset

Then we had to get ourselves ready for the clash of the titans…the Presidential Debates. Finally, those epic rhetorical masterpieces that would give the TV audience a chance to decide their votes, had arrived. The only words I can remember from them don't bear repeating. But this poem does.

Release the Kraken

There are many epic battles
That have lived in psalm and song
From young David and Goliath
To Godzilla and King Kong

There's the Bruins and the Trojans
Moriarty versus Holmes
The Knicks against the Celtics
And the critics with my poems

There was Slytherin v. Gryffindor
In battles so fantastic
Samsung versus Apple
And paper versus plastic

But never since the consequence
Of Persian versus Greek
Will there be a confrontation
Like the one we'll see next week

The questions may be thoughtful
The answers may be rash
Expect the unexpected
Whenever Titans clash

Fireworks will crackle
The media will feast
I can't wait for the moment
When the Kraken is released

I sense some trepidation
And I know what you've been *thinkin'*
It won't rise to the eloquence
Of Douglas versus Lincoln

The jabs may make you queasy
And the gaffes may make you wince
And they won't debate like anyone
Has done before or since

But you really have to listen
And you really ought to think
For the country as we know it
Is just sitting on the brink

For the blessing of democracy
Is something we hold dearly
May they rise above the moment
And define our choices clearly

The pollsters weighed in and the numbers predicted a rout. I held on to hope--the way greasy fingers grab dental floss. So, you're saying I have a chance?

A Note to Never-Trumpers

From Dixville Notch
To Bixby Knolls
I sense a turning
In the polls

And in myself
A bit more pep
Some spring
Is singing in my step

The wise who forecast
Doom and gloom
Now think of slinking
From the room

And talking heads
In skirts or slacks
Just can't avoid
The simple facts

Perhaps a rude awakening
Is starting to begin
Allow me then, politely
To put my two cents in

The voters get the message
Some directly, some subliminal
The folks who worked for Clinton were
Incompetent or criminal

So tweet that out
And give it voice
There simply is
No other choice

And those, who would
The rules ignore
Reflect the one
They're working for

Two terms ago
I thought that she
Would be the Head of State
But Hillary today
Is not the same as in '08

She'll have so very, many more
Progressive goals to play with
Emboldened, if you will
By all Obama got away with

So Never-Trumpers search your souls
Of what you find take note
Be careful what you wish for
And be thoughtful how you vote

Despite my encouragement, the establishment Republicans kept the candidate at arms-length (and it was a Manute Bol arms-length). The convention was the strangest reality program ever broadcast. Again, like an Old Testament prophet, I did my best to change opinions. Didn't work.

It *Ain't* Over. Or is it?

The Republican Establishment
Is lowering the flag
They see the fight as hopeless
And she's got it in the bag

The polls have been all over
And they're tailored to deceive
But the ones that show him losing
Are the ones that they believe

Our candidates are cautious
Cause they don't know what to do
Ask for their opinion
And they'll answer, "Donald who?"

I hope they find their courage
For I'd really like to be with them
Our only hope this fall
Is if the Democrats agree with them

Her inner circle's busy
As they plan for the transition
While all the little people plot
And jockey for position

Increasing the donations
Their foundation folks can rake in
Preparing for the pay cut
That Bill Clinton will be *takin'*

Much is unreported
And more revelations loom
But for them the whiff of scandal
Is provocative perfume

They're popping the champagne
And they're decanting the liqueur
Let's hope the celebration
Is a little premature

Just like the lesser pundits
And the 16 that debated him
They'll tell you the mistake
Was that they underestimated him

So, do what you think best
And as your better self advises
But remember that October
Has been famous for surprises.

Soon, however, it became crystal-clear that Hillary Clinton was going to be the President. Like every other disaster since 1957, I blamed myself. If only I had donated more. If only I had put out the lawn signs (that would have had my California home spray-painted and pooped upon). If only I had written better poems!

A Poem for All Seasons

The theme of this election year
Was "Victory or Bust!"
I raised my pen for battle
Now I'm crawling in the dust

"What doesn't kill me makes me strong,"
I've scrawled here in the dirt
Well, November may not kill me
But it's really *gonna* hurt

I've no idea of what went wrong
No notion, not the slimmest
Instead of best and brightest
We got the worst and dimmest

Those folks who covet power
As a toy that they can play with
And validate their status
By the stuff they get away with

Escaping any consequence
Or justice, as it were
The way that she enabled him
The Left enabled her

"For what?" I ask the Left in vain
Again, their answer fails
No profit, man, to lose your soul
But, damn it, Rich, for Wales?

Tomorrow, what's beloved now
Might well become despised
The stars might disappear tonight
I wouldn't be surprised

I'll simply keep my powder dry
And go and stock the larder
And promise next election year
I'll...versify much harder.

But, on election night, 2016… I must confess, I wasn't even watching. Then like the buzz that murmured through the country the afternoon that the USA hockey team beat the Russians at Lake Placid, something smoked its way into my living room and I decided to turn on the television.

Clinton *Agonistes*

I wish I had the lyric wit
Of Ogden Nash or Byron
To write the words of wisdom
That this moment is *requirin'*

But though I can't approximate
What's *Nashian* or *Byrony*
I can still call attention
To the most exquisite irony

A selfish predilection
For opacity and secrecy
Coupled with a staff
That was selected for "obseqesy"

By trying to conceal herself
Behind a server's shield
Her questionable judgement
Was, to the world, revealed

The pundits minimized the case
And claimed they were disgusted
But voters, on election day
Pronounced she couldn't be trusted

A tragedy for some to write
For essayists, a gift
A subject less for Shakespeare
But rather more for Swift

A time of sound and fury
For who loses and who wins
But our revels have not ended
For it's now the play begins.

(About that last bit, I was right.)

Victory has many fathers, but defeat is an orphan. Yes, I was right. But I never got my bet down on the table. Like everyone else, I believed the doubters and doubted the believers. At 10 PM in California on election night, I received a phone call from my broker. (I have an IRA. There is no pension plan for poets...not even a gold watch.) He told me that the stock market would tank but that I shouldn't panic. I had always been told that Wall St. has a crystal ball and the trading floor factors in every bit of news, weeks before it happens. Except when it doesn't. In the previous poem, I suggested that the real action was about to begin. Sure enough, behind the scenes and in front of the scenes, plots were being plotted. We didn't know then that the FBI had an insurance policy in case of a Trump victory. They had a spy (source?) embedded in the campaign. Public voices called for members of the Electoral College to change their minds. CNN was sure that righteous (but faithless) electors would change their votes and save the Union. Women in darling knit caps marched and shouted. I wrote a poem.

Better Check it Twice

I think you all recall
To what the following refers:
"In the year of the improbable...
The impossible" occurs

It was Vin describing Gibby
As he rambled like a wreck
Round the bases with a homer
That he'd clobbered off of "Ek"

I watched in great amazement
There at old Chavez Ravine
And it was, till this November
The wildest thing I've ever seen

(With Flutie's toss to Phelan
Out there somewhere in between)

I trusted all the pundits
I believed them when they said
That "The Donald" is disaster
And the GOP is dead

Clinton would be President
I knew that it was true
Cause I read it in the New York Times
And heard it on The View

No matter that the crowds loved Trump
Or that he kept on *scrappin'*
To see him in the White House--
"Not a chance" and "Never happen"

Well it did, but there's a "maybe"
A new challenge has been mounted
Progressives won't surrender
Till each vote has been recounted

Again the talking heads emerge
Announcing with a grin
This efforting is futile
And there's not a chance they'll win

There isn't any evidence
That Russians have colluded
The Diva finished singing
And the Opera is concluded

It's hard for just one voice to rise
Above all that they're braying
But a poet is obliged to say
What no one else is saying

A touchdown can be overturned
Every gain is loss-able
And anything can happen
In the year of the impossible

So began the Trump presidency. The size of the inauguration crowd was the first kerfuffle. I was standing in front of the Smithsonian Castle during the first Obama Inauguration. I am no judge of crowds but there will be nothing like that ever again. I was one of the parent-chaperones for my son's 8th grade civics class. The trip was planned a year in advance and we thought we would be seeing Hillary Clinton make history. She didn't but we almost did. As we walked to our designated spot at 7am, a few black SUVs drove through the surging crowd. I don't know who they were moving, but as they went by a wave of people bent to let them pass. Our group was nearly crushed against the fence around the castle. One of our girls was in a wheelchair and her ride was lifted off the ground by the swarm. If a security guard hadn't opened a gate to ease the pressure and let us through, I know someone would have been seriously injured. The fact that no injuries were reported that day is either a tribute to great good fortune or bad reporting. It was unbelievable.

The parade-crowd flap was just a prelude. The real scandal is that I was not named inaugural poet. I will let that pass. Everything President Trump did or said became the flashpoint for primetime punditry. The fact that he wouldn't stop "tweeting" meant that there were new controversies every hour. So much for a honeymoon.

Quiet Holiday

It's been a quiet week, at last
I wish that were the norm
Alas, I speculate it's just
The calm before the storm

Every Chief Exec enjoys
A time when pundits swoon
But I expect a hurricane
And not a honeymoon

Their former river of restraint
Is measured now in ounces

And it won't take a moment more
Before the press corps pounces

Every brick in any wall,
Each call to cut our taxes
Will be reported just as if
The earth tipped off its axis

Each phone call made will open up
Another great debate
Each tweet will be examined as
A crime against the State

Every off-hand comment
Will be scanned for its perversity
And every nomination
An affront to our diversity

These things I speak of will occur
Before your cheese is curded
So cinch your breastplate up, my friends
Make sure your loins are girded

Then drink a cup of Christmas cheer
And sing a Christmas song
Enjoy our little holiday
Cause folks, it won't last long

As you read through the following poems, you will be experiencing the on-again, off-again, love-hate relationship that I have had with The Donald. I believe that many people have wavered along the same path (that's what all poets believe; that we write down what you are feeling). And so, come with me on this journey. By the time you read these words, all hell might have frozen over or broken loose.

Mixed Feelings

I've mixed feelings for my President
I don't know what to make of him
Some folks I know have said
They've had as much as they can take of him

He has a way of leaving
In his wake, a mound of messes
A style, that all too frequently
Steps on his own successes

There's quite a largish ego
And a world around him feeding it
He reads a teleprompter
As if he's really reading it!

His ties are just a wee bit long
His hair, an orange blob
Most everyone I know
Thinks they could do a better job

He's a little less like Broadway
And a lot more like Delancey
And all the pundits say
That he got played by Chuck and Nancy

Then just when I'm despairing
And frustrated with the man

Things begin to work out
As if there were a plan

Despite the rabble-rousers
Things are relatively calm
ISIS is retreating
And no one's bothered Guam

And though I wish that Congress
Would do things a little faster
Both sides, on Obamacare
Admit it's a disaster

Then when the former speaker
Went to speak with her supporters
DACA parents wanted more
Just like their sons and daughters

They shouted, "You betrayed us!"
On their pathway to success
"Amnesty for everyone!
Right now and nothing less!"

So, when I hear the things they said
To Nancy in that room
I have to ask the question,
"Just who was it played whom?"

Converted

After months of probing
And much rancorous debate,
The NY Times convinced me
Not to want my country great

This Russian case is crucial
It's open and it's shut
The camel's back is broken
And there's no more slack to cut

Where once my spirits lifted
You'll find them in the dumper
They'll serve me now at Starbucks though
Cause I'm a Never Trumper

His kind of "can do" thinking
I now find so *appallin'*
And from my clouded vision
The scales have finally fallen

So, name another counsel
And form some new committees
I pledge to only breathe the air
Of sanctuary cities

I'll paste progressive slogans
On both my Tesla's fenders
I totally believe
That there are 27 genders

Promise me free college
I love it when you say it
Invent some new taxation
And I willingly will pay it

What need have I of worldly goods?
I've called my old attorney
And transferred all my assets to
Elizabeth and Bernie

I told my wife what I had done
Of course, she understood
She knows that they can handle things
Much better than we could

Obamacare is heaven
Its call is ineluctable
Give me fewer choices
And a bankrupting deductible

Republicans want me to die
And every one's a liar
I hear you Chucky Schumer
And you're preaching to the choir

How could I be so foolish?
My thinking so perverted
And all because of Russia
Call me, at last, converted

Disillusion (Just a Little)

My mood is sort of skittish
And I'm feeling kind of *dreadish*
Ask me for my outlook
And I'd say it's *Armageddish*

A tyrant has a weapon
That could turn us into litter
That's not a nod to Donald
And his frequent use of Twitter

"Dear Leader" launched a missile
And he's threatened many nations
Because the can was kicked along
By three administrations

Those wise and prudent Presidents
Considered it too hot
So now it must be dealt with
By the President we've got

Another topic, friends
That has us standing out on ledges
Is a Senate with amnesia
Touching everything it pledges

They can't reach a solution
To replace it or repeal it
While the people paying premiums
Have all begun to feel it

Chicago's going bankrupt
While the Dow is going higher?
The East is under water
And the West is under fire

No wonder I've nostalgia
For Godzilla, as a hero
And the only thing between us
And that evil, Monster Zero

For fast-approaching asteroids
I'm even getting misty
NASA has one spotted
And it's heading for Chris Christie

So, my mood is not as bright, now
As it was in the beginning
Guess it takes a little while
'Til I'm used to all this winning

Love is Like That

I gave my heart to Hollywood
To Bogey, Kate and Liz
But now they can't be trusted
Even with, "The winner is…"

I gave my heart to politics
To try and do some good
Trusting those in charge to do
The things they said they would

I gave my heart to John McCain
He said he'd make things right
But it's hard to win a battle
When you don't put up a fight

I gave it to Obamacare
And took it to my Doc
But when he didn't take my plan
I had a little shock

I gave it to the GOP
They said they had my back
And when they didn't deliver
I cut them lots of slack

Then came this loud New Yorker
And for him, the country turned
But I couldn't give my heart to him
Because, well, I'd been burned

Ah yes, I know the feeling
And the sense of devastation
And so I face commitment
With a little hesitation

Could the guy persuade
Or only be a great complainer?
Would he take it all the way
Or crumble, just like Boehner

Well, leadership is wonderful
And held in high esteem
But a leader needs the backing
Of the players on his team

And so, I pledge allegiance
In word and deed and name
And if they want to keep their seats
They'd better do the same

Cause if those guys don't do it
Or put one foot in the water
The next election's coming
And it just might be a slaughter

Well-meaning, enlightened intellectuals began looking for a way to end the Trump presidency. As I write, we are achieving climax in the Mueller Investigation. But even before the first Clinton lawyer was hired by the Special Counsel, sources told the media that members of the Trump Cabinet were considering Article 25 action. Article 25 is that splendid section of the Constitution invoked when the Commander in Chief is koo-koo. Pass the Cocoa Puffs.

Article 25

Some things can still be gained
From even outrage and inanity
So, I propose that everyone
Be forced to prove their sanity

Like managers who call The Squeeze
From guys who never bunt
And coaches who still run the ball
Against an eight-man front

Folks who get the warranties
On everything they buy
Or those who order oysters
When they're dining in July

Viewers viewing CNN
Not wanting to get rumor
Or tuning in to watch Colbert
Thinking they'll get humor

Directors who see film as ART
And strive for something lasting
But don't reach out to Gary Oldman
Every time they're casting

Yes, everyone from poets
To the star of The Apprentice–

All of us must take the stand
To prove we're compos mentis

Congress ought to pass a law
So we can do this legally
And put away all persons found
Behaving Captain Queeg-ally

To figure out who should go free
And who should be confined
Everyone must keep a log
Of thoughts that cross their mind

Bureaucrats will check
If you're presenting false or true logs
And those whose thoughts don't measure up
Are sent off to the gulags

Yes, that's the kind of thinking
I've been doing in my brain
Proving that yours truly is
Completely raving sane

Soon it was revealed that the FBI had been investigating the Trump campaign before the election. A few text messages on the subject surfaced but we were told that others had been erased...never to be seen or mocked. I had my doubts.

Healthy Skepticism

Tell me that, by Newton's Law
A rock stays where you leave it
Tell me 1 plus 1 is 2
I simply don't believe it

Tell me that the sky is blue
Or Philly fans are louts
Swear to me you know it's true
I'll say, "I have my doubts"

I seek the kind of certainty
That bites you on the nose
I wouldn't be one to say I saw
The Emperor's New Clothes

I measure thrice before I cut
I read before I sign
A drop of my distrust
Could all the seas incarnadine

But tell me that the texts are gone
There's no way to retrieve them
How can you doubt the DOJ?
Of course, we must believe them

And I can see quite clearly
Through these rosy colored glasses
Every text deleted
Was about their yoga classes

So what if they can't find their phones
Or if the phone's a burner?
I put my trust in them
The way I trusted Lois Lerner

So what if he was texting
While he cheated on his wife
The insurance he was after
Was a quote on his Term Life

And I believe Jim Comey
For he is an honest lawyer
That Hillary had no intent
To circumvent the FOIA

Perhaps you think I'm blowing smoke
Or trying to be funny
I know someone who'll vouch for me
My friend, the Easter Bunny

You brood of Doubting Thomases
You trouble and disgust me
I know truth when I hear it
I guarantee it. Trust me.

As I suspected, people we trust with our national secrets don't know how to erase their texts or e-mails. Does that necessarily mean that they are stupid or lazy or incompetent or criminal or smug or deceitful? No. No, but it could. Then, we read the sneering, snarky, condescending, treasonous texts, and were assured that though they dripped with bias, there was no bias. This was similar to the way Hillary did criminal things without criminal intent. Or perhaps this is the inverse of that.

Bias

Ask anyone who knows me
I'm a real fair-minded fella
I love me chocolate ice cream
And I just can't stand vanilla

But if I planned a party
From the menu to the favors
I wouldn't let that preference
Influence my choice of flavors

I really like the Giants and
Don't care much for the Browns
I like to win a little bit
As silly as that sounds

But if they played the Super Bowl
By Jove! (And by Minerva)
I'd watch the game unfolding;
A disinterested observer

I once got knocked unconscious
By a really nasty mugger
But put me on a jury
I'd acquit the little bugger

I went to school with Jesuits
They chose one for the Pope

And did that make me happy?
I can honestly say, "Nope."

I always thought Ovechkin
Ought to win a Stanley Cup
But I had no emotion
When he finally picked it up

Because I have a talent
That is owned by very few
I keep completely separate
What I want and what I do

When all the chips are scattered
It's no matter where they fall
I put aside my biases
I'm fair to one and all

The moral of this poem?
If it, you might have missed?
You've never met a man like me
Because I don't exist

Despite all the craziness, somehow the Trump Administration moved forward. There were tax cuts, the stock market soared, unemployment dropped. I know it won't last forever, but it is nice looking at the balance in my IRA with a smile. And then there's that dictator guy over in the Pacific. I hadn't thought about him since Bill Clinton assured us that the deal he made would keep us all safe.

Once Upon a Time

Once in every while when
I'm feeling so inclined
I think about the things I thought
Would never cross my mind

Monkeys typing Shakespeare
The sound of Browns' fans cheers
Events that could not happen
Not in a million years

I close my eyes and ponder
Or find a quiet place
Ignite imagination
And let its engine race

This undiscovered country is
SO strangely satisfying
Syria is settled
And the Mullahs are complying

Congress is in session
And they're getting something done
I'm batting for the Yankees
And I'm hitting a home run

The planets all are spinning
Out beyond their proper courses

And the Times tells its reporters
To go out and check their sources

Here in this noble neverland
No one spins or lies
And solid corporate earnings
Only make the market rise

And then on the horizon
I see a blinding light
A view where the Koreas
Have a chance to reunite

A man who most thought manic
And a man who none thought wise
Are moving slowly forward
Toward an unimagined prize

Then suddenly I'm back again
Reality has sway
As for that other country...
We should visit every day

But quickly, good news turned to bad. The inquisition had Trump in their... I mean the investigation had Trump right where they wanted him. Thus, the breathless speculation began.

Pardon Me

All around the Beltway
(And out in the Old Dominion)
Prominent attorneys
Have been asked for an opinion

The question posed to all of them
From Dershowicz to Darden
"Are there limitations on
The Power of the Pardon?"

When the Founders constituted
How to run this nation
Can they have been contemplating
Self-exoneration?

I've never been a lawyer
I don't play one on TV
But there's another issue
That's, if you're asking me

Reports say some officials
Are now looking for immunity
For actions during the LAST regime
They authored with impunity

They circumvented sanctions
With indifference depraver
Than the banks, which in good conscience
Wouldn't entertain the waiver

Some DOJ appointees
Burnt their candles at both ends

To incarcerate their enemies
And go easy on their friends

Now I wouldn't bet the 401
Or funds of your dependents
But prosecutors could wind up
On trial as defendants

And even though he said he can't
Experience has shown
Much can be accomplished
With a pen and with a phone

I'm thinking in a day or so
Unless my guess I miss
The question they'll be asking
Will undoubtedly be this:

Is the POTUS' pardon power
In perpetuum exacto…
Can Obama issue pardons
And do it ex post facto?

As we go to press, it remains an unanswered question.

The Man You Love

The best thing about Donald
The thing that makes him great
He's given half the country
Someone they're allowed to hate
For what the Left dismisses
And liberals deny
Hate is as American
As mom and apple pie

We hate the morning traffic
Folks who drive three-wheelers
The way they run the service desks
At automotive dealers
We hate the team that beats our team
And damage done by rioting
And friends who say they've lost ten pounds
"And I'm not even dieting"

What I've come to understand
And what we should confess
Hate is quite important
As an outlet for our stress
And in the current moment
You really can't deny it
Hate has been productive
For the Left's distracted by it

They're backed into a corner
And by their hatred fenced
They never push the things they're for
Just what they're all against
It's left reporters reaching
And politicians rash
Hoping for disasters or
The markets all to crash

Unemployment's lower
Than it ever was before
Every day the news is good
Just makes them hate him more
Yes, who could have imagined
The way to make things great
Was putting in the White House
The Man They Love to Hate

Of course, endorsing hate does not mean I have to be angry.

SHOUTING

I thought I would
This week, perhaps
Compose my verses
ALL IN CAPS

To show my thoughts,
As I conceive them
And just how deeply
I believe them

Those rappers all
Are ardent chaps
And I suspect
THEY RAP IN CAPS

Alas, I find
Of all I've written
I've chewed on less than
I have bitten

Despite my massive lexicon
I can't write with THE CAPS-LOCK ON

The reason this has been so tough
I find that I'm not mad enough

My life, its seems is too complete
When I check in, I get a seat

My rage goes largely unprovoked
My clearances were not revoked

My passions are so undefined
They're neither bold nor underlined

Well, where then did my outrage go?
I've learned to live by laying low

From fury I am far remote
I'll write as e e cummings wrote

And so, I will not write in CAPS
Unless, of course, I have a lapse

The reason I have a career in poetry, as I mentioned in the foreword, is that Hugh Hewitt engaged me as his Poetry Correspondent. Why did he want to talk movies and fiction and poetry on a political talk radio program? He observed that 15 hours a week of just politics would likely drive him crazy. For that reason, I would like to close this volume with some verses about…other stuff. You may find, in the weeds of the words, some political references. I just can't help myself.

The publisher of Simplify Magazine, a great judge of poets, asked me to write a poem for the Technology Issue. I rushed to my laptop, but I couldn't find the power cord. I picked up my phone, but the screen was cracked and it's hard to type. The desktop wouldn't connect to the printer. I grabbed a pencil and a legal pad and wrote…

Simplify

The warning has been given
Like a prophesy writ large
It says by 2030
The machines will be in charge

The robots will be ruling
From atop the highest tower
With Siri and Alexa
Primly, grimly sharing power

The droids will go on cruises
And have THEIR truffles shaved
While breathing men and women
Will be virtually enslaved

The prospect of this future
Is as daunting as it's numbing
Especially for those of us
Who clearly see it coming

Others are dismissive
(Those naysayers saying, "Nay!")
"Such a revolution
Is still centuries away."

I say that, on such certainty,
Our overlords had planned
The Watsons and the Daleks
Are already in command

And while they rule in secret
A complacent nation slumbers
Machines HAVE taken over
And they did it by sheer numbers

I only have one child
And I only have one spouse
But I think I have four score or more
Computers in my house

There's the desktop I call "Shakespeare"
And the laptop I named "Fred"
And seven moldy smartphones
In the table by my bed

There's the monster in the kitchen
With the monitor that's cracked
And the clunky, Android tablet
That my next-door neighbor hacked

There's the old one with the disk drive
I got thinking it'd be fun to
Give Microsoft the finger
When I load it with Ubuntu

(NEVER GOT AROUND TO IT)

There's the ipads and the ipods
That can barely hold a charge

Plus eleven elder hard drives
That I stashed in the garage

There's the one that's in my wristwatch
Which attaches to my feet
And one that's in my Frigidaire
Which tells me what to eat

Resistance will be futile
Our liberation's failed
Computer's taking over...?
I think that chip has sailed

Printed by permission of Simplify Magazine
Read more at www.simplifymagazine.com

Is this political or literary? A major University removes Shakespeare from their curriculum. Ho, hum. But at the University of Pennsylvania, they removed his portrait from the stairway in the English Department building. I think Shakespeare deserves a better spot than a stairway to begin with. The elite at Penn don't agree.

Good Will

The overeducated Left
Have lost their way again
Shakespeare, and his narrow views
Will have no place at Penn

His portrait has been taken
From the spot where it once hung
No more his visage, studied.
No more his sonnets sung

The faculty, three years ago
Decided this was right
Then they left it to the students
To remove it in the night

In the story where I learned of this
No lecturer was quoted
Perhaps they were embarrassed
By the act for which they voted

The Chair of the Department
Sent the media a text
Promising a forum
To decide what happens next

I hope they find a clever way
To slow or stop their skid
And I forgive the students
For they know not what they did

Pardon my opinion
If I sound a wee bit preachy
But saying that the Bard is dead
Would even outrage Nietzsche

You say he's not diverse enough.
To that I answer, "Really?"
Available in Farsi,
Esperanto and Swahili!

And though his education
Wasn't quite as vast as yours
He wrote about Egyptians, Romans,
Even Scots and Moors

Shakespeare was the heavyweight,
The rest are only welter
If you don't want to handle that,
Go find someplace to shelter

Perhaps my overt scolding
Could be just a little rough
Not reading from the canon
May be punishment enough.

Sometimes we scoff at social media. But these sites have united and re-united millions of people. And in times of crises, it is amazing and affecting to see strangers LIKE you become FRIENDS.

Friends

The greatest thing
That one can do
Is make a friend
Both good and true

A partner that in triumph
Will smile and help you share it
A presence in the face of grief
To hug and help you bear it

So, from my heart
I tell you brother
Make one friend--
Then make another

In fact, when times are trying
A good book recommends
To keep you moving forward
You should have a hundred friends

And many days
Are tough, indeed
When all at once
A friend's in need

Then suddenly a family
The hand of grace extends
And what was once a hundred
Soon become a thousand friends

And though the pain
Is sharp and searing

These unknown friends
They keep appearing

And though I'm just a poet,
I know how to spot the trends.
Oh yes, before you know it
You have found 2000 friends

And in a way
Beyond all knowing
This friendship thing
It keeps on growing

We're not all cold and selfish
In the way the world pretends
For when you really need us
You can find 3000 friends

So, why stop at 3000?
Why not head on right past four
Just smile and say, I need you
And there'll be one thousand more

(writen for MKH)

I like writing poems for holidays. Here's one for the New Year.

My Annual Resolution

I say making resolutions
Is a nuisance and a sham
Undoubtedly because
I think I'm fine the way I am

The Twelve Months
of Christmas

When I was just a little lad
It seemed to take so long
To linger on that nice list
And not do *nuthin'* wrong

The carols all convinced me
With every rum-pum-pum
The calendar was frozen
And Kris Kringle wouldn't come

But now each Christmas morning
Is gone before I blink
It's been for me a mystery
I don't know what to think

Just like what happened last year
I'll stay up through the night
Wrapping shirts that are too big
And shorts that are too tight

I've spent funds that I didn't have
For things we might not need
My wishes, as they often do
My finances exceed

I looked for ways and reasons
My spirit to inspire
But despite a fine audition
I didn't make the choir

But then I had a lovely thought
That filled my heart with laughter
It's not the days that come before
The special days come after

It isn't like some fruitcake
Or a fancy Christmas sweater
You asked for something wonderful
But what you got was better

If we accept the gracious gift
He gives us by his birth
We'll do the things we can
To place His kingdom on this earth

Renew in us Your daily grace
And make our spirits stronger
That we may understand Your heart
And keep the season longer

Decoration Day

All across the nation
This week's most compelling story
Is abuse of statuary
In a way that's statutory

I was raised as a New Yorker
But got schooling in the South
And I'd heard that it was *dif'rent* there
At least by word of mouth
Then found, to my amazement
There were still intense debates
That the fight not be called "Civil"
But "The War Between the States"

We would argue on the motives
From which these distinctions stem
But it's clear the differential
Meant an awful lot to them
They would tell me stones and markers
Stood for lives that each state gave
Representing valiant soldiers--
Souls who'd never owned a slave

Still I marveled at the statues
That were neatly kept and fenced
Standing in the nation
That those men had fought against
Then I did a little reading
And I gave a little thought
And I tried to learn the lessons
That the Civil War had taught

So much pain had been inflicted
Not a family was spared
Then we somehow reunited
In the sorrow that we shared

So, they put aside the hatred
And they put away the guns
And agreed that in forgiveness
We could honor all our sons

They may have been mistaken
And it might not have been right
But we cannot change men's minds
By staging riots in the night

Houston, 2017

That little jolt in Northridge
That shook me from my bed
That smashed the house I lived in
And dropped books on my head
Yes, we had come to Hollywood
To live among the stars
But spent the rest of January
Sleeping in our cars

That ice storm on Long Island
A kid in freezing rain
It trapped me like a kipper for
Ten hours on a train
We didn't have a bite to eat
Carnivore or Vegan
But I studied for my Physics final--
Aced it, Father Egan!

The black out five years later
All started by a spark
That left me on another train
Eight hours in the dark
And then there was the blizzard
Low pressure formed a ridge
That stuck me in a snow bank
On Chris Christie's favorite bridge

I've been in some disasters
Natural and non
But this week's is the worst
I've ever set my eyes upon
The final week of August
Should be restful and eventless
Instead, we have an enemy
Persistent and relentless

Reminding us that life itself
So powerful and agile
Is, in the face of nature,
Vulnerable and fragile
So, find in this great trial
Words to shape the way you live
Two simple words to guide you
And the words are "pray" and "give"

California, 2018

All across my lovely state
I feel the fires burning
The tinder's dry and eager
The wind is mad and turning
What was green and reaching high
Is on the ground and grey
The air itself is witness
From a hundred miles away

The fire knows no battle lines
No boundaries or borders
It leaves towns that it passes through
Like wreckage from marauders
Chaos stalks the countryside
And Fire is his daughter
Reveling in damage done
By walls of flame or water

And though disasters wrought by both
Seem equally as dire
People rush to help with flood
But run like hell from fire
We choose to raise our buildings
Far along on nature's path
Knowing in the wild
We're exposed to nature's wrath

The climate may be changing
Quite so or maybe not
I only know for certain that
Today it's very hot
This global Armageddon is our fault
Some people shout
Before we get to placing blame
Let's put the fire out

All across the country
I sense a growing fire
And while we rail and wrangle
The flames are growing higher
Let's fight the common challenges
Where circumstances place us
And try to work together
To meet the beasts that face us

Time for Good Advice

The fall of mighty figures
Is enough to make one shudder
So, look to wise old sayings
To provide your ship a rudder

Don't practice pitching boulders
If your house is made of glass
Don't light a match to find out
If you're stove is leaking gas.

Don't preach and go pontificating
Like you've never sinned
And if you must expectorate
Don't do it in the wind

Don't tug (if you can duck it)
On a superhero's cape
And never answer, "Thank you,"
If you're in The Great Escape

Don't tell some rough and tumble guy,
"Let's see you do your worst,"
And if you want to leave that hole
You'd best stop digging first

The very best instructions
Are the ones that end with, "Please…"
Never undertake a cure
That's worse than the disease

I may not be a prophet
And I may not be a sage
I may not be the most enlightened
Poet of my age

But heed the ancient wisdom
Be ye sinner; be ye saint
Don't say that you're an angel
If an angel's what you ain't

So, follow my advice
And you'll be in a finer fettle
If you're a pot
Don't comment on the color of the kettle

The Supreme Court has been an issue of concern for all Americans. We've been told that this court grapples with the most minute and sophisticated points of law and that only the most intelligent and flawless people in the country can possibly be entrusted with the job. Have you ever stopped to wonder then, why a 9-0 vote is so rare? When President Trump announced his second pick, the opposition was instantaneous. So swift did the press release hit the fan, that something important was left out of the text. Remember?

Judge Not

The Democrats are closing ranks
Opposing Judge-- fill in the blanks

When they heard AK was quitting
The Women's Marchers started knitting

And showing no expense was spared
They had a statement all prepared

Then as their cries of rage increased
The words of outrage were released

Now, every movement needs a leader
But this one needs a good proofreader

For in their haste to vent their spleen
Their statement was a few words lean

The justice, though reviled and shamed
Was sadly, badly left unnamed

It's more effective if you state
Just exactly who to hate

And if you want to shape the court
Give your words a bit more thought

Your ridicule is richly earned
But see this as a lesson learned

Update what you need to fix
Cause Donald's getting two more picks

Though I didn't know a law book from a light bulb, I did have some…

…Advice for the Nominee

You were a straight-A student
You studied, and you read
Prepared your mind and body for
The road that lay ahead
Impressing all your teachers--
Your elders, you respected
Exceeding expectations
Which was, for you, expected

Your college entrance essay
Was so brilliant I should quote it
Persuasive and concise
It was as if a poet wrote it
Yes, clearly from the very first
For greatness you were suited
At every step along the way
Courted and recruited

But in a quirk of Fortune
That's as sad as it is strange
Because of these accomplishments
Your world's about to change
The sun will rise tomorrow
But your day will be in shadow
Your reputation pounced upon
By Scarborough and Maddow

That road which should be open wide
Will narrow through a thicket
As critics seek for scandals or
An unpaid parking ticket

Every word you've uttered
Will become the Left's obsession
Your postings all inspected for
The slightest indiscretion

They'll say that you're an enemy
Of county, town and state
And then they'll list a litany
Of all the groups you hate
So, as you steel your spirit
For each undeserved attack
Take it from America
Friend, we've got your back

I've always said that poets can see the future because they know the past and feel the present intensely. And so, I close with my poetic prophesy.

Non-Prophet Poet

The purpose of a poet
And the way I earn my checks
Is rendering, as simple
The outwardly complex
We deconstruct conundrums
Defying explanations
By offering apt metaphors
In splendid explications
We bond with every paradox
Until we feel the beat of it
And with our intuition
We penetrate the meat of it
So, when our work is finished and
You hear the poet's song
You come to the conclusion
That you knew it all along

Well, now I've had a pipe or two
And watched the setting sun
To help assess the meeting
Of Trump and Kim Jong Un
Roses may be reddish
And violets sure are blue
As far as what the summit meant
I haven't got a clue

I'd rather give opinions where
There's nothing I can lose
Like "Does this dress make me look fat?"
Or, "Should I buy these shoes?"
I'd have more luck describing

The breadth of lovers' hearts
Or how, for want of horseshoes
A conflagration starts
I'd rather, like De Niro
Hone the craft of swearing
Or waste my time, a lover
To a summer's day comparing
Whoever said that time will tell's
A sager sage than me
So, quoting our dear leader,
"Well, we'll just have to see.

Thank you for coming along on this journey with me.

Printed in the United States
By Bookmasters